BLUE LINE K-9

Puppy Training Made Easy

15 Easy Steps to Have Complete Control of Your Dog in Any Situation

by Michael J. Soler

Puppy Training Made Easy:
15 Easy Steps to Have Complete Control of Your Dog in Any Situation

ISBN: 978-0-9908442-0-4

www.blk9.com
Email: info@blk9.com

Give feedback on the book at:
feedback@blk9.com

Printed in U.S.A

Contents

Introduction

The Beginning

As a young boy, I was always interested and close to animals. You could always find me playing with my friends' and family's pets. The desire to work with dogs began when I started teaching the family dog some fun tricks. Luckily, our family dogs were very good sports.

At the age of 17, I joined the United States Marine Corps. This gave me the opportunity to work with military working dogs.

After the military, I became a law enforcement officer with the Cecil County Sheriff's Office. While there, my interest turned into a passion for working with dogs. With the support of my wife, Tara, I began taking training courses and became a certified dog trainer and mentor trainer with Animal Behavior College.

Wanting to share my knowledge and passion with others, my wife and I opened Blue Line K-9, Inc. in 2007. As I began to train more and more dogs, I saw the need for further education. I found many training courses and apprenticeships, traveling all over the country to expand my knowledge and training techniques. I constantly continue to seek out new methods and theories in dog training, but thanks to a dog named Charlotte I developed my own philosophy and method of training.

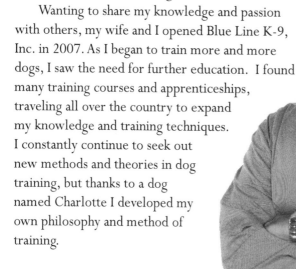

In 2008 while on an apprenticeship in North Carolina, I worked with a female Belgian Shepard Dog also known as a Malinois named Charlotte. Up to this point I thought that the best dogs to work with had to be German Shepard and male like my dog Bruno, but I was mistaken.

Charlotte as well as the thousands of other dogs we have worked with proved to us at BlueLine K9 that "all men (dogs) are not created equal" and "all roads (or trainings) do not lead to Rome (Controlling your Dog)".

I realized traditional methods would not work for Charlotte although most worked for Bruno. I was at a standstill using traditional methods so I started reading and watching every book and DVD I could get my hands on. As soon as the DVD was finished I would put the new knowledge into practice.

I then called Bruno and off we would go to practice. I could see it in his eyes, "Dad is at it again." Bruno is such a good sport. Bruno taught me more than I could ever teach him. To this day, I still try new ideas with Bruno.

Through my work with Bruno and Charlotte I developed my own training methods and philosophy. That training method and philosophy is based on redirection and positive training.

My training is based around the theory of Pavlov's Classical Conditioning. By creating a conditioned behavior using an unconditional response, you get a well behaved dog. Now, Blue Line-K9 and my training methods have expanded and we are very pleased to help others train their pets on a much larger scale.

Our goal is to help you have a positive and fun adventure enjoying your dog in any environment! Training your dog does take time, patience and commitment that will be well worth it in the end!

Michael J. Soler

TO BE SUCCESSFUL IN TRAINING YOUR DOG TO DO ANYTHING YOU WILL NEED THE FOLLOWING:

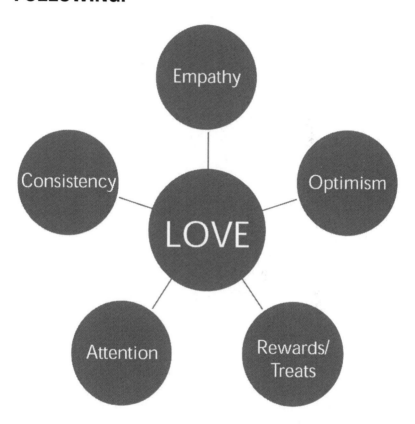

STEP 1:

Understand the Philosophy

My philosophy is based on years of experience in helping owners and their dogs have a better understanding of a positive process that reduces unwanted behaviors and allows a trusting, enjoyable relationship.

Positive reinforcement and redirection allows you to communicate clearly with your dog. You decide what you want your dog to do, and let him know what you want by rewarding him when he does it. When you reward your dog for doing things correctly, he's more likely to repeat those good behaviors.

For most of us, our dogs are our friends and companions. They are a part of our family. Positive reinforcement can help reinforce our connection we have with our dogs. Positive reinforcement helps build the bond between you and your dog by strengthening the trust between you.

Much like people, dogs appreciate being told they have completed a job well done as opposed to being told they were bad. Aren't you more likely to do a better job for your boss if he tells you he appreciates your work when you do a job well done, instead of just coming to you when something could have had a better outcome?

The theory that best describes our philosophy is based on Pavlov. Ivan Pavlov born in the year 1849 in Saint Petersburg, Russia was a physicist that was interested in the behavior of both humans and animals. Pavlov was a behaviorist. This means that his theories were focused on behavior that could be observed. Behavior can be measured and thoughts cannot. Pavlov thought that you can observe what goes on in the mind and what comes out of the mind. Pavlov studied reflexes, those automatic behaviors that are caused by a stimulus from the environment. Some reflexes, such as blinking your eyes when a puff of air comes in it, or the sucking of a baby when something is put in his/her mouth are considered automatic reflexes.

Pavlov conducted experiments on dogs by ringing a bell and immediately rewarding the dog with a piece of food. After a period of time, and much repetition Pavlov rang the bell and withheld the food and the dogs began to salivate in anticipation of receiving the food.

Pavlov repeated this exercise with the dogs over and over again. As time went by the dogs began to associate the food with the ringing of the bell. When the food was removed, the dogs continued to anticipate the food when the bell was rung. Conditioning is really a matter of repeating an exercise over and over again which will result in a predictable outcome. Repetition builds predictability and reliability.

Dogs learn by association. From a training perspective, this is very valuable information which can be used to help you communicate more effectively with your dog.

By emphasizing the positive actions of your dog, it will encourage the continuing development of your dogs' skills and abilities. Positive reinforcement is usually much more effective than trying to force improvements by dwelling on the negative. By consciously emphasizing positive actions, your dog/puppy will rise to the occasion and will try to please you to the best of his ability. By focusing on the positive you can encourage greater growth and success for you and your dog.

Redirecting focus from a negative or unwanted reaction, whether predicted or already occurring, is an incredibly useful tool to help manage behavior in dogs. Positive training focuses on teaching the dog an alternative behavior instead of punishment. This allows the dog to learn valuable coping skills which start with redirection. We can aid their success by thinking ahead and either avoid situations that trigger negative behavior or create other things for a dog to do where positive behavior is encouraged.

If certain situations are impossible to avoid, then it is vital that you observe your dog carefully and give him something else to focus on in an uncomfortable situation. For example, if you have a dog that lunges at other dogs, people or moving objects as they go past, give your dog an activity to do rather than allow him to focus on something that elicits the negative reaction. This is done most effectively before your dog gets to the point where he feels the need to react. Redirection is therefore most effective when used before your dog reacts. If he reacts negatively before you have a chance to redirect him, gentle removal from the situation is the best way to get him into a state where he can learn again.

Using positive reinforcement to train your dog means you are rewarding the behaviors you like, and ignoring the behaviors you do not like. You can use treats, praise, or toy rewards.

STEP 2:

What is Re-Directional Training?

Redirect to better behavior

This type of training is easy on you and your dog. It makes it easier to learn, but you do have to use your brain. Ask yourself, "What did I do to reinforce my dog's behavior and what is the best way to get him to stop?" Many times it may be easier to yell, but as you continue reading you will see that is not the best way to solve the issue. We want to train with our brain, not pain!

Let's go over a few simple ideas:

1) Behavior that gets rewarded gets repeated

Whether the behavior is a good behavior or an unwanted behavior, if it is rewarded it will continue. For example: You come home and your dog jumps on you. You yell at your dog to get down. You are rewarding the behavior and your dog would rather be yelled at than ignored. So each time you come in the dog will jump. Now on the flip side, if you come in and your dog jumps and you ignore the behavior, the dog will soon think, "Wow, dad is not happy and is ignoring me, I better stop jumping." This leads us to the second idea:

2) Behavior that is not rewarded will most likely stop

When you come home and your dog jumps on you, ignore the behavior and the dog. You then do something else for 10-15 minutes until your dog relaxes and calms down, then you can pay attention to him/her.

3) Continuous reinforcement

Once you establish a behavior, continue to reinforce it to make it stronger. Continuous reinforcement by using praise or treats will help develop the behavior quicker.

4) Set goals for you and for your dog

Reinforce the behaviors you like. Make a list of what is important to you as far as your dog's behavior and the environment you live in. Is walking on a lose leash important? Is sitting quietly for dinner important? Think about what you would like and what is important.

One of the keys to success is having your dog be successful without the fear of failure. If you have not told your dog what is expected then you can't be upset at the behavior.

If you really want to change your dog's behavior, you must be willing to first change your behavior. When you change your behavior, your dog will learn new ways to respond and please you. If you keep doing the same old thing, you will keep getting the same response.

3 STEPS TO ACHIEVE BETTER BEHAVIOR

1 **Teach your dog expected behavior**

Teach your dog how to appropriately get your attention by sit, place, lay down

2 **Ignore unwanted behavior**

Do not make any sound or reward unwanted behavior

3 **Reward behavior you want and expect**

When your dog offers up the wanted or expected behavior, reward with praise, treats, or affection

STEP 3:

Understanding Your Dog

Your dog in photos

Dogs see in photos. Each event that occurs in your dog's life is retained in their mind like a photo. Your dog has a photo album in his mind.

Since dogs learn in photos, it is easier to train them when they are young. Up to six months is the easiest. As they get older, we have to erase the old photos and create new ones. This takes time, patience and consistency. Dogs are constantly learning. It is up to you to make sure that your dog is learning the right things.

If your dog is 4 years old and for simplicity, let's say he keeps 1 photo a day. That would be 365 x 4 = 1460 photos. That is a lot of photos to have to sift through. Consider the example below...

Let's say your dog has been jumping on the sofa every day for a year. He would have 365 photos of, "I jump on the sofa and lay on the soft cushion." Now, you would prefer that your dog does not jump on the sofa, so we need to create a new image. We would create the new image by making it uncomfortable for your dog when he jumps on the sofa. You would do this by placing carpet runner (the plastic kind that has the sharp tabs on the back) upside down on the sofa. When the dog jumps up, the new photo would be: "I jump on the sofa and, Oh my, there is something sticking me when I land." You have just created a new photo, and the dog should not continue to jump on the sofa.

So the goal is to create new positive photos of the behavior that is expected for your dog.

Understanding your dog's behavior

Before you attempt to teach your dog or puppy anything, you must first understand, or at least make an attempt to understand him. If you understand how dogs operate, how they think and what motivates them, you are well on your way toward having a meaningful impact on your dog's behavior and improving your relationship.

The two of you can work together to understand the needs and wants each of you may have. Let's face it, we have issues too, but no matter your issues, YOU are the boss! Understanding your dog begins and ends with understanding and knowledge of who is in charge. So much of all dog training-no matter which type of training you are engaging your dog in- is about communication and understanding.

Let's look at some critical elements of dog behavior including their reliance on thinking as part of a pack and their need to have an alpha dog in their life.

Think like a pack

How do dogs think? They think as part of a pack. As part of your family, they are part of a pack. Remember that dogs are descended from the original pack- the wolves. Dogs still think they are part of that pack even though they are far removed.

There will always be a pack leader. If you make sure that you are the pack leader, you will be able to control your dog in any situation.

Understanding how a pack operates, means understanding that your dog operates as part of a hierarchy. He needs to know that someone is in control. Be aware that your dog not only needs but demands this standard of hierarchy.

Applying a pack mentality to your relationship with your dog means providing leadership. By acting like his leader, your dog can instinctively relax and fall into the role of "family pet." In fact, without leadership dogs can become very confused, anxious or dominant. A dog that knows his place in his human pack is a happy dog. A dog that does not is a confused dog and can exhibit many unwanted behaviors because of it.

Many of us think that dogs want to be leader of the pack, but the reality is that most dogs do not want to be the leader. They want to be part of the pack.
They want to know someone is in charge and controlling the household and establishing control or structure. It is your job to provide that control or ensure that someone in the household provides it. If nobody in the household steps up and establishes a clear leader role and

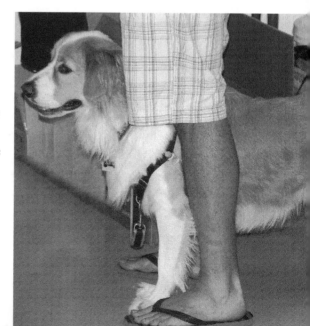

hierarchy, your dog will take the reins and establish himself as leader of the pack. That is when trouble happens. Your dog understands that this is survival. If no one provides the leadership, the pack can't survive. A dog that questions his place in the household pack may suddenly display destructive behaviors. The dog becomes confused, he starts taking his anxiety out on your house/stuff.

What does a pack leader do? A pack leader has many jobs:

- Decides where the pack will go
- Decides where the pack will eat
- Always walks in front
- Decides how the other members of the pack behave
- Decides who is allowed to bark and when
- Decides who can play and when
- Can take anything from any dog and claim it as their own

A puppy is in no position to make big decisions. As a puppy, there is a lack of experience (i.e., no photos to make good decisions).

The psychology of the alpha dog

A leader must be established and it should be you! Even if you do not establish yourself as an alpha type, you should at least outrank your dog. There is no other way to train your dog than to out rank him. Even if both of you are at the bottom of the totem pole, he should rank below you.

How can you establish yourself as your dog's leader? In the dog world the higher-ranking animal goes first. You want that higher ranking animal to be you. So, your dog should eat after you do, and he should walk out a door after you do. Never let him run past you—out of a car, into your yard, or into the park. It's that simple. Make sure that no matter how cute and adorable he looks when trying to be disobedient you do not let him know that you think he is adorable. Rather, continue to establish yourself as the leader who must be obeyed.

➡ Make him get down from the couch so you can sit, even if there is room for you to sit elsewhere. Doing this reminds him your needs come first.

➡ If your dog is allowed to sleep on the bed at night, on occasion, make him get down. Again, your comfort is the priority, not his.

➡ Do not feed him until after you have had your meal no matter how hungry he appears to be. He will survive his hunger and you will benefit by reminding him that you are the boss.

➡ **Sit:** Your dog should get in the habit of sitting for the good things. Ask him to "sit" —get excited and praise him when he does—before putting down his food dish, before petting him, and before letting him walk out the door on a walk. He'll start to think all good things come from you, but only The very definition of routine is doing something over and over again. The very definition of establishing behavior is yes, that's right, routine. So, provide that routine and follow that with positive reinforcement. Do this over and over again and you will see results, we promise!

Your behavior

Yes, your behavior is just as important as your dog's! It is time to establish your leadership in order to further demand respect and attention of your dog. This includes:

REINFORCEMENT

You should give your dog as much positive reinforcement as possible. This means providing a consistent routine. Provide a consistent routine over and over and over again. Positive reinforcement is a must. Mark your dog's good behavior with wild enthusiasm— "YES, good boy or girl!" Show them that you loved the behavior. We like positive responses and so will your dog!

Dogs are excellent students and one of the hardest things to understand is that they will quickly learn exactly what you teach them. This means the good as well as the unwanted. Most of the time it is us, as owners, that teach our dogs the wrong behavior. Not on purpose, but it happens.

Remember, any behavior that is reinforced will be repeated. Hitting, yelling, jerking the leash is still reinforcing your dog. If this is the only time you pay attention to your dog, your dog will repeat the behavior to get your attention, any attention. So, by praising your dog when he does something you want or like, that too will be a repeated behavior. Your dog wants to please you and wants attention. Let's make it a good experience all the way around!

At first, you may only make small steps. Small steps, successful steps will win in the end for you and your dog.

ABUSE

It is easy to get frustrated when teaching or working with your dog, whether it is where to do his business or learning to sit, but abuse is never the solution to any problem.

 Do not hit or attack your dog in any way no matter how frustrated you become.

YELLING OR HITTING YOUR DOG MAY CAUSE THE DOG TO HAVE:

When you get frustrated and lose your patience with your dog, he will begin to fear you and it will become hard for him to concentrate and learn what you are trying to teach. Not only have you committed a form of abuse, but you have also created a more difficult environment for the both of you to live, love and learn. Fear and respect are not the same thing. Fear will push your dog away and it will not bring you any closer to having an obedient dog. Displays of aggression only teach dogs to be defensive and therefore aggressive, when abused.

If at any time you fear you may hit your dog or abuse him in any way, seek help. Call a local dog trainer to help you with the mission you are trying to undertake, or talk to your vet. If you turn to abuse, you will forever impact the relationship you have with your dog.

What if your dog makes a mistake?

It is natural to make mistakes during the learning process. Just think about it; you take a course in playing the guitar, you will not be perfect the first time and although you will get better there will be times you make a mistake. Imagine if you were yelled at or punished for forgetting a chord. There would be no way to avoid the punishment if you do not have a memory that can remember a hundred percent of what you learn. Look at your expectations and have patience. Your dog will make mistakes.

If your dog makes a mistake, stop for a moment and take a look at the situation. The first thing to consider is, "Did I make a mistake?" Check to make sure you gave the correct cue and that your dog understands the cue you are giving. We want to end the training session on a positive note so try again to get a successful result.

What can I do instead of saying "No"?

In our society we are blasted with the word no from the time we are babies all through adult life. No, we can't do something, or no, you can't go somewhere. If you are caught in a "no" trap when working with your dog, instead of saying no, give a command, like sit or down. That gives your dog something else to focus on, instead of the inappropriate behavior.

STEP 4:

Building Value and Setting Goals

Teach your dog the value and the respect will follow. I can already hear the question "How do I do that?" Through much trial and error on my part, I have the answer.

Make Yourself PRICELESS to Your Dog!

h him

➤ **Teach your dog that you are the value and you control what he loves and use those things to reward him. Teach your dog what you do want, not what you don't want.**

For example: If you take your dog to the park, but he loves other dogs and people so he ignores you and forgets that you exist, what did you teach him? You taught him that you do not exist so he does not have to listen to you because the other things are more rewarding. He needs to be taught the skills and master them before you can take him out.

If you control what he loves and use those things to reward him, he will listen. What if you go back to the park but make him sit for a few minutes before he is allowed to play. You have taught him that you are the boss! **Be Consistent** – If you do not like a behavior, do not reward it.

Praise

➤ **When you see your dog doing something you like, praise him. Let your dog know what makes you happy. Be enthusiastic and excited.**

Give boundaries

➤ **Your puppy/dog should not be making his own decisions. Boundaries help your dog understand what is allowed and what is not allowed.**

What are the rules of your house? Every household has rules that need to be followed. If you have children, they know what is expected of them and what is acceptable and so it should be with your dog. You can't just expect your dog to know what is right and wrong. He must be shown. Decide what the house rules are and stick to them. Let him know that even though you're the nicest person on earth and the best human he could ever hope to find, your house does have rules, and he must follow them.

This is instilling a "no work, no reward" program. Your dog learns to recognize that You are in control of everything in his life — feeding, playing, walking, trips in the car, etc. — and that those things come with a price attached, whether it is a "sit" or "down." Refusal to obey a command results in no payoff.

This can also be explained as fear of loss. Fear of loss is simple. The dog wants something, but if he does not behave properly, it will be taken away.

A classic example is when someone comes to your door and the dog bolts to the door. The dog wants to see who is there. He may be barking and scratching at the door then, when you open the door, he bolts out of the door.

By having rules, he has to sit by the door until you give the ok to go out. The fear of loss is that he wants to go out. If he is not behaving, he will not be allowed to go out. This is **"Fear of Loss."**

Another example: you are walking your dog and another dog comes towards you. Your dog wants to meet the dog. He is pulling and tugging on the leash. You back up away from the dog because tugging is not acceptable. **Fear of Loss:** you are taking him away from what he wants—the other dog.

Setting goals

WHY IS IT IMPORTANT TO SET GOALS?

Setting goals helps to organize our thoughts; it gives us an idea of the ground we need to cover and the direction we need to go. If we do not set goals, whether in life or dog training we have no direction. Things will appear to be haphazard and we will usually fail. Goals help us see how far we have come and our successes.

Blue Line K-9 wants you to succeed! Go get some index cards and write down your goals for you and your dog. Every day pick one or two goals to work on.

MOST IMPORTANT GOAL...

The first and most important goal you should have for your dog is: **NAME RECOGNITION.** Your dog needs to know his/her name and needs to know to respond when you call the first time.

Other goals you may have depending on your needs are:

1. Loose-leash walking
2. Sit
3. Down
4. Come or let's go
5. Place
6. Control in and out of doorways and cars
7. Potty training
8. No jumping
9. Tolerance of children and other animals

You may have noticed that we do not have "stay" on the list. Why, you ask? Remember dogs see in photos. If you think about it, what would a stay look like? If you were asked to draw "stay" what would it look like? It would look like a sit, down, place or stand. There is no clear photo for a "stay."

Once you have set your goals and worked towards meeting them, revisit them and keep track of those that you have reached.

TIP

Remember there will good days and bad days. One day your dog may seem to understand everything and the next can't remember anything. There are many reasons this may happen. It will help if you go back to your goals, look at where you have started and what you have accomplished. It helps to look at what goals have been reached and what areas need improvement.

For example: Your dog is excellent with come but has not quite mastered sit. Check to see if you have practiced sit as much as you practiced come.

STEP 5:

Markers

A marker is a word that is used to 'mark' or immediately indicate the moment a dog is correct with a behavior. Like when the moment the dog's bottom hits the floor in a sit, you would use the word "YES" telling the dog that was the right behavior. A marker is followed by reinforcement with food

and/or verbal praise, or affection. The marker creates a brief separation between food or touch and the behavior, so food is a reward not an enticement. Here is an example:

- You ask your dog to sit
- Dog's bottom hits the floor
- You respond with an enthusiastic **"YES"**
- Followed immediately by a treat or praise

If you want to use a word as your Marker, make sure it has these specific characteristics:

- Short and sharp.
- Comes naturally to you when you are happy.
- You don't use it too often in other conversations around your furry friend.
- It can't be confused with other commands or your dog's name.

We strongly suggest the word **"YES"** as a marker word. The reasoning behind using "yes" is that it is always a positive word.

The word **Yes**: is a **Positive** word that isolates a moment in time. This word or sound releases the dog from the position or from focus.

A "Motivator" such as food, toy, or affection is paired with the marker word (in this case, we are using yes as your marker word), which encourages the dog to repeat what caused us to give him the treat, toy or affection. This method allows your dog to be a willing participant with an upbeat attitude. The greatest benefit of training in this way is that your dog's mind "stays open" and engaged. This engagement is absolutely necessary before learning can occur in any subject, humans included. Eventually, you will move away from using treats and work with praise and affection.

Since dogs see in photos, think of the marker as the shutter button on a camera. The moment your dog offers a behavior, you want use the marker to take a picture of that moment. He'll then remember that behavior because the marker lets him know he's going to be rewarded for what he just did.

This can be a powerful tool if trained and used correctly because it can **speed up communication between you and your canine friend.**

STEP 6:

Treat Training

Treats for reinforcement will work well if your dog is food motivated. That is why treats work best for puppies. As your dog gets older he may not be motivated by food and you will rely on praise and affection.

Dogs, like people, like to please themselves. When asking your dog to do something, the first thing he may think of is "what is in it for me?" When we regularly reward our dog with a job well done, they will want to work for us, much like you and your boss.

One important thing to remember is a behavior that is rewarded is repeated. If you reward your dog for doing something right, he will do it consistently. A reward is presented after a behavior has been completed correctly. You are not so much rewarding your dog for 'being good' you are reinforcing a correct response making it more likely to happen again. Treat training can be referred to as "positive motivational training."

➤ **Treats simply help you to get the behavior you want from your dog, and let your dog know that he performed the behavior correctly.**

A reward will only increase behavior if it is desired by your dog. It is a great idea to have a variety of treats – some favorites, some less so – that way, your dog will not be able to predict what treat he may get next. Variety will keep your dog hoping his favorite treat may be the next one.

If you don't want to be overly reliant on treats you need to use other effective rewards for your dog. The most important of these is praise. Every time you treat your dog you should also praise him with specific and genuine praise in a voice that tells him he's done the right thing. Treating as you praise will condition a higher value to your praise so that even if you don't treat some of the time, your praise will have a positive reinforcing effect.

When training a young puppy with treats, it is important that we don't create a dog that enjoys food more than praise from his owner. As the dog gets older and treats continue to be used, the result will be a dog that listens pretty well when the treat is the best option around. We want the dog to value you and your affection.

The treat should be a very small (pea-size or even smaller for little dogs), soft piece of food, so that he will immediately gulp it down. Don't give your dog something he has to chew or that breaks into bits and falls on the floor.

➤ Carry the treats in a pocket or fanny pack.

➤ Do not show the dog the treat before you ask the command, wait until it is completed.

➤ Each time you use a food reward, you should couple it with a verbal reward (praise). Say something like, "Yes!" or "Good dog," in a positive, happy tone of voice. Then give your dog a treat.

Is a treat a reward or is it a bribe?

A treat can be a bribe or a reward depending upon when it is given. Timing is everything.

If you have your dog's attention and ask your dog to complete a command and he does it, you then take the treat out of your pocket and offer it, that is a reward.

If you are offering the treat up front, the dog sees it, and then you make the command, this is called luring or bribery. It is not a reward. You are telling your dog that you have a nice little treat if he performs a certain command. Bribery can also take place if you ask your dog to perform a command that he knows how to do and has completed the request over and over but for some reason just is not in the mood. You have asked a couple of times and you decide to take the treat out of your pocket and show it to get the desired outcome. The treat has now become a bribe. The goal in training is to avoid bribery!

Before asking your dog to do something, have his attention and be sure he is looking at you. It is important that your dog knows his name and responds to it. Teaching your dog to respond to his name first will prompt him to look at you when called. Then you can ask him to perform his task. After the task is performed, the treat and praise are given. Now that is a reward!

STEP 7:

Impression Training

Impression training is used to provide new photos to your dog combined with your dog's fear of loss. Confused? Let's talk about this.

Let's say your dog likes to bolt out of the door every time it is opened and this is an unacceptable behavior for you. The dog has a picture of when the door is open, he runs out and you stand on the porch jumping up and down screaming at him to come back. You may even chase him down the street so, to the dog, this is a game.

How do we correct this? When you open the door and see the dog heading to the door, you close it. When you open it again and he still wants to go out, close it. If he gets part way through, close the door applying pressure and he will back up.

Your dog wants to go out. By you closing the door, you are creating the "fear of loss" of what your dog wants. Eventually, with practice, your dog will sit at the door when it is open and wait for you to give the command that it is ok to go out. This may take some practice and patience on your part.

You are now creating a new photo. When the door opens, the dog knows if he wants to go out of the door he has to wait for your command, giving the dog what he wants.

Think of it like a flash card. When we were in school, we practiced learning words, math and other things through the use of flash cards. We saw them over and over until we committed them to memory. Giving your dog a new impression (photo) is like using flash cards. You may have to practice the new behavior over and over but the dog will have that moment when everything clicks and the new photo/impression will stick.

STEP 8:

Distractions

In life, we are constantly distracted and so is your dog. The best way to start training your dog is in an area where there are distractions. Why? In life there are always distractions. Think about it. You have an important report to get to your boss, the phone rings, or other people need your attention. Your dog has distractions also. By training in an area with distractions, when you get home it will be much easier to practice. Let's face it, when walking your dog, you will see other people, dogs, animals, all are distractions. If we teach the dogs with distractions it becomes easier to work with your dog in the backyard. A distraction is something that gains your dog's attention so that he is no longer concentrating on you.

The key is to use distractions to your benefit when you are training. By building a solid relationship and making sure your dog knows you are the most valuable person in the world the distractions will not

affect them anymore. Use distractions to help build the value.

Effective training incorporates interruptions and distractions into each lesson. If you introduce the right disturbance at the right time, your dog will learn to stay focused and listen to you regardless of what is going on around them. Remember training is not a set time.

For example: We were taught in school that one plus one equals two. And we know that one plus one equals two at home, in school, at work, and at the grocery store. Dogs, however, do not necessarily make the same generalizations. Your dog might learn that "sit" means "lower your hips to the floor while keeping your front end up and hold still" while he's in the backyard. But he doesn't know that "sit" has the same definition in different places unless he is taught in different places. After he's exposed to a variety of locations and distractions, and is required to sit in all of them, he might then learn that "sit" is the same everywhere he goes.

This is why it is very important that your dog knows his name. When you call, he turns and looks at you, regardless of the distraction.

It goes back to building "value." Build a strong foundation/relationship with your puppy or dog and they will live to "please" you.

STEP 9:

Introducing Commands

Sit

Down

Come

These are only 3 of the over 250 commands you can teach your dog. It is important to be specific and consistent with the commands to teach your canine. Do not overlap your commands.

SIT is one command with one objective and one photo.

DOWN is another command with a different objective and a different photo.

SIT DOWN could cause confusion for your dog. The photos don't match for them.

Tell me if this sounds familiar. You want your dog to get down off the couch and you give the command get DOWN. Your dog then goes from the sitting position on the couch to the laying down position still on the couch. You then start to get mad because you want your dog to get down from the couch, not lay down on the couch. You give the command again a little louder this time believing your dog didn't hear you. Your dog looks at you through partially open eyes wondering who you are barking at. This situation could go on for hours.

You as the leader need to step back and realize that your dog has done exactly what you asked him to do. You gave the command DOWN and he saw the photo for DOWN and gave you what you asked for.

Your dog is very smart and wants to please his leader. Have you taught your dog more than the 3 commands listed above? Did you create a photo for OFF? You might use that command for when you want your dog to get OFF the couch or OFF the counter, etc.

No matter what commands you introduce, always remember the 3 keys to success:

Patience, consistency, and practice!

Training equipment

The training equipment list is short and sweet. Make sure you have these basics before you start training.

1. **Marker:** We at Blue Line K-9 recommend the word "Yes" as a marker. A marker is a signal to the dog that he has done something well. Markers should be followed by a reward.
2. **Motivators or rewards:** A motivator is something your dog likes and will work for. Food can be a great motivator, but if your dog is not food motivated, you can use a favorite toy or affection.
3. **Collar:** The best type of collar to use is a flat cotton or leather collar.

4. **Leash:** One 6-foot and one 15-foot flat leash, cotton or
    leather. While we are discussing leashes, let's discuss the use of
    a retractable leash and why they are not a good fit for training.

RETRACTABLE LEASHES

Retractable leashes are bulky and do not give you control over
your dog. They can also be dangerous, snapping and flying back hitting
you or your dog, causing injury, or the cord could get tied around your
hand, finger or dog cutting off circulation.

Name recognition

Most people believe the first thing they should teach their puppy
or dog is walking on a leash, however, the very first thing you should
teach your dog is its name. Name recognition is key. If you have to call
your dog's name more than one time to get their attention, your dog
either does not know his name or if you call by name multiple times,
feels he does not have to respond to you.

Now that you have everything you need, you will start by luring
with a treat, when the dog goes into the position of the command,
state the command mark with YES and release the reward.

Once your dog has mastered the first command, it's time to
introduce another but continue to practice the previously taught
command.

Always end the training session on a positive note!

STEP 10:

Leash Control

A leash is a guidance tool!

Here is a list of items you will need for leash training:

1. 6-foot lead
2. 15-foot lead
3. Treats
4. Patience
5. Consistency
6. Practice

Learning how to use a leash correctly is vital in building a healthy relationship with your puppy. What is even more important is remaining consistent with your leash training. If you are not consistent in using the leash you will probably have a difficult time in training your puppy.

Puppies have a short attention span. This is normal. They may also have difficulty focusing attention on the training. This is one of the reasons why the leash is an effective tool. It is much easier to regain your puppy's attention if he is not running off!

It is very common for people to hold on to the leash too tightly. Many people feel they have more control over the leash the tighter they hold it. Generally this may cause more discomfort for your dog and the result will be the opposite of what you want to achieve. A dog will struggle to go forward. You struggle to go back. This is a yo-yo syndrome. When holding a leash the goal is to have as little control as possible in order to control your dog. It is about applying pressure, but not yanking or pulling backwards. The goal is to have your dog walk on a loose leash.

How to hold a leash

Most people will usually wrap a leash around their wrist; however, that can add pressure on your wrist and actually cause damage to you. The best way to hold a leash is to take your non-dominant hand and place your thumb through the loop. If you feel you want more control, wrap it over the index finger and under the middle finger. You can then make a loop and either shorten or lengthen the leash as needed. Make sure the leash is under your pinkie and this will create a natural leverage lock. (See pictures below)

Incorrect: *Leash wrapped around wrist, which may cause internal damage.*

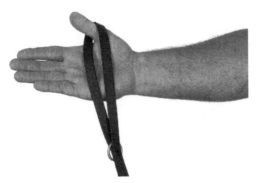

Step 1: Thumb through loop hole.

Step 2: For better control, loop over your index finger.

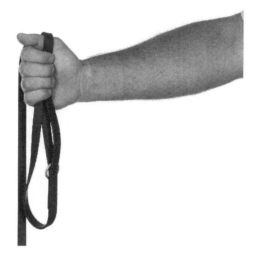

Step 3: Close hard.

Step 4: Walk your dog.

Most people do not realize that their less dominant or involuntary side is actually the stronger side. The dominant side is the weaker side.

If you are curious as to how this works, it involves our voluntary and involuntary muscles. A voluntary muscle is one you must consciously choose to move, such as when pointing your finger or picking up a glass. An involuntary muscle is one that moves without you choosing to move it, such as breathing, and muscles involved in reflexes such as eye blinking.

Let's say you want to take Fido for a walk. You attach the leash to the collar wrapping the leash around your dominant (voluntary) wrist and off you go. All of a sudden, Fido spots another dog and with a tug of the leash he is pulling in a different direction. This is an example of your voluntary muscles. The dog tugs and your voluntary side says, "Whoa, Fido is pulling I must follow" as Fido pulls you down the street.

Now, let's look at this same scenario using the non-dominant side. You attach the leash to Fido's collar and take the leash placing it over your thumb of your non-dominant (involuntary) hand, making sure it comes under your pinkie to form a leverage lock. Off you go down the street. Fido sees another dog and he pulls. As he pulls (your involun-

tary side says, "Whoa, you are going to tip") you instinctively hold your place, placing pressure on the leash and giving you time to call your dog so he looks at you, and he is now distracted from the other dog.

Our goal on learning to walk your dog on the leash is to walk with a loose leash. Your dog needs to learn that when he pulls on the leash, he gets nowhere. If he wants to continue walking, it has to be by your side on a loose leash. Don't pull him towards you, just call him by name, say YES (with enthusiasm) good boy/girl and reward him when he arrives. Then start walking again with your dog by your side. If he starts to get ahead of you, call his name, as he looks at you praise him, and continue on your way. Just remember that if he starts to take off call his name, once he responds, give praise and keep walking. Now, if he sees a squirrel or other interesting item and takes off, start walking backward, applying pressure but not pulling on the leash. As soon as you have your loose leash, start walking again.

Loose-leash walking

When walking it is best to have a 12-15 foot lead. This will give your dog the idea that there is some freedom and he is not attached to your hip, but still gives you control.

When teaching your dog to walk with a loose leash, keep it from being boring. Going in a straight line is boring! Change your pace, make some left and right turns, go in circles but do not be predictable. Make this fun by rewarding your dog for following your hand. Use your marker word of "yes" and give a treat or affection.

If your dog is not paying attention, play a fun game of keep away! If your dog is still not paying attention and starts to go forward, stop and apply light pressure and start to walk backward, turn around and change your direction. Your dog will soon wonder where you went and try to catch up to you. If he looks to the left and thinks you are going to start to go that direction, go to the right.

When he catches up and the leash is again loose, reward him with praise and a treat. You want your dog to pay attention to you, not you paying attention to your dog. You want him to think that unless he keeps an eye on you he never knows which way you will turn. It is simply about wanting him to learn to keep his eye out for where you are going. He should notice immediately when the direction is changed. The moment you notice he is not paying attention, go the opposite way before he pulls on the leash. This should be fun! He should think that the object of the "game" is to watch you and stay next to you.

This is a training exercise. Don't expect to go on an actual walk with a destination. You will be changing your direction and turning around often so understand that distance is not the goal. Walking in a straight line is BORING!! Keep him interested by changing your direction, making a circle to the left or to the right, throw in some left and right turns. Make it fun and exciting for your dog so your dog will never know what is coming next and he is more likely to pay attention to you.

If he drifts off and looks like he is going to begin to pull, go the other way. If you are having problems, ask yourself if you are boring him to tears, and if the answer is "yes," then make it fun for both of you.

STEP 11:

Housebreaking

So, your puppy needs housebreaking. They all do. Relax; with some basic skills and knowledge under your belt, you will have this under control.

Basics

The basics begin and end with patience. No matter what method you use to housebreak your puppy, you must be patient, understanding and consistent. Learning to go outside to do his business is one of the hardest things your dog will ever learn. Like children, some will take to house training/housebreaking easily and others may be a bit more challenging.

Some people do not worry about housebreaking their dog. They may feel that most dogs will at some point mess in the house so why worry about it. The puppy may go inside or outside. Not a big problem, why worry about what is natural, right? Others may figure that if they pay attention to when the puppy needs to go out, they will be able to get him outside and prevent any problems. Of course, this may be a dangerous plan.

The reality is that unless you want to clean up messes on a regular basis it is worth the effort to housebreak your puppy. With the right effort at the right time it can be relatively easy to housebreak your puppy.

This chapter will cover:

1. Understanding your dog's behavior
2. General housetraining/housebreaking methods
3. Stubborn dogs and other problems

1) Understanding your dog's behavior

Let's face it, housebreaking a puppy is necessary. This is something that needs to be accomplished as quickly as possible.

Much will depend on the dog's temperament. Some dogs will want to please and will be happy to learn the rules of the house (which means not doing their business in the house), while others will challenge you until you just feel you can't be challenged anymore.

If you understand your dog's basic temperament, his canine nature and what motivates him, you can quickly learn how to work with (not against) him to achieve success.

If you know how to condition your dog properly and if you are patient, consistent, and determined, you should be able to house train your dog in record time.

2) General house training/housebreaking methods

Now that you have established yourself as the leader of the pack/ the alpha dog, you are ready to train your dog to do his business outside, not on your carpet, your furniture or your-ahem- shoes.

Most people use crate training to housebreak their dogs, but there are other less well known methods that are successful and we will discuss all of them.

Before choosing a particular housebreaking method, remember to consider your dog's age, temperament, and general ability.

While puppies can learn by whatever method you are using as long as you are consistent, patient, positive, and dedicated. Older dogs are going to need much more care, love and patience. You CAN teach old dogs new tricks! The key is to have patience while "relearning" old patterns (or photos). It can be done, so be positive!

CRATE TRAINING

The most common and most often taught version of housebreaking is crate training. It involves the use of a crate, clear rules and a lot of patience.

Here is how this technique works:

Your dog spends a good deal of time in the crate. The crate environment is seen by him (and you) as a doggie bedroom of sorts.

Dogs won't use their living space as a bathroom, so this ensures that your dog or puppy won't mess in the crate. This method is particularly effective with puppies.

Crate training is the method most espoused by dog experts, mostly due to its simplicity and effectiveness. Patience and consistency are very important and key to successful house breaking.

CONFINE YOUR DOG TO A SMALL ROOM

Even though many dog trainers, breeders and experts may suggest crate training, not every dog owner may want or like the idea, so another method is to simply confine your dog to a small space or room.

This method requires even more diligence on your part because your dog may or may not see the room as his space that needs to be kept clean and protected.

If you use this method of training you also might want to keep a schedule and prepare for accidents. As with a baby or small child, dogs relish being on a schedule. So, put your dog on a regular schedule using the bathroom (backyard). This method is best suited for a person that is home a good deal of the time because keeping to the schedule all the time, every single day is essential.

PAPER TRAINING

It may be old fashioned but many people swear by this method of housebreaking.

Quite simply, your dog is trained to go on the newspaper. This is not the cleanest or most effective way of housebreaking your dog, but some people use it with great success. It requires a desire and willingness to clean up after the dog frequently. Also it is necessary to be patient and persistent about putting the dog on the newspaper.

Don't assume that if you don't have a puppy, you can skip the puppy stuff and move onto the older dog stuff. All dogs can benefit from crate training and other housebreaking methods because your home is new to this "new-old" dog.

Here are some general tips that can facilitate your dogs housebreaking regardless of the method you choose to use:

➤ **No drink after 9pm:** Do not let your puppy drink water after 9 p.m., even f your household retires early. This will prevent night time potty trips. Of course, if it is very hot or your dog is excessively thirsty, you may give him ice cubes or a small amount of water.

➤ **Get rid of parasites:** If your dog has parasites or worms, take him to a vet. You do not want your dog to have parasites or worms as this may cause additional issues and it is best to get it treated quickly. Your dog's ability to be successfully housebroken requires that he be healthy and able to control his urges.

➤ **Keep his diet regular:** If your dog is suffering from constipation or diarrhea, it will be difficult if not impossible for him to adhere to a strict housebreaking schedule. Make sure to keep his diet health and regular so there is no stomach upset.

➤ **Reward and praise:** One of the critical components to any training schedule is the need to keep your dog happy by being generous with the praise. Praise your dog often. Every time your dog cooperates by peeing outside, pooping outside, or asking to go outside, heap generous amounts of praise on him and he will step up the efforts to please you.

➤ **Keep your dog happy:** If your dog does not get much attention or attention only when you are working on the housebreaking, then it is unlikely you will be successful. Dogs, like children need attention, any attention. If he does not get positive attention, he will seek to get attention any way possible, even if it is negative. Make sure you play with your dog and give him good solid, generous attention so he does not need to act out to continue getting the attention he wants.

3) Stubborn dogs and other problems

When to train: As soon as you bring your puppy home, is the time to start training. It really needs to be that fast.

Ideally, your puppy will begin the housebreaking process by the time he is 8-12 weeks of age. How long it may take you to completely train him will be determined by a variety of factors. These factors include the type of breed, his need to please, his intelligence and your diligence and patience.

Breeds: Some breeds are more of a challenge than others. Some breeds are easily distracted and others are not so eager to please. Some breeds considered a little more difficult to housebreak are:
➤ Beagle
➤ Dachshund
➤ Whippets
➤ Most of the terrier breeds (Jack Russell, Irish Terrier, West Highland Terrier)
➤ Pugs

➧ Bassett Hounds
➧ Shih Tzus
➧ Pomeranians

Do not assume that because you may have one of the more challenging breeds that you will have a problem-you may have the exception to the rule.

Temperament: Even within the context of a breed, a discussion of temperament is essential. Your dog may come with some built-in qualities of the breed but within breeds there are differences in temperament. Just like children, many dogs come with their own set of behavior standards and abilities.

Get to know your puppy as soon as you can. Is he eager to please or a bit less concerned with how you perceive him? Does he listen well, and take to training or is he a rebel bucking authority every chance he gets?

You can't control these inherent temperamental tendencies but you can take them into account as you try and housebreak your puppy. Keep in mind that dogs that have rebellious and stubborn tendencies may take longer to train. Dogs that are eager to please and quick to learn can be trained in a blink of the eye.

How long will it take?

How long it takes to housebreak your puppy will depend on your dog and your efforts. If you have a puppy that is easy to train, you are clear with your method and apply the right principles your puppy could be trained in a week or so. Most puppies will take between 2-4 weeks to fully train.

If it should take longer than that, consider your efforts and the technique you are using. Do not switch techniques, but make sure you are being firm, patient and consistent.

Particular challenges with the puppy

Puppies are fun, goofy and busy. These attributes can make for some challenges. Remember that your puppy is easily distractible—even a bit of attention deficit if you will—and that if the rules are not clearly defined and enforced the puppy will push the boundaries of appropriate bathroom spaces.

In addition, puppies have to go to the bathroom often. Once they realize it, the need to go is NOW! Puppies are babies; they can't control their urges like an older dog can

This is not about breaking your dog's spirit. Your dog can be every bit the puppy even when housebroken and have some basic obedience skills.

To be effective you must be firm, patient, and consistent to break your puppy of bad habits and do so in a way that is kind, gentle and reassuring. That IS what we are teaching! These are the most import attributes a puppy parent can have when housebreaking.

Let's move on to the details of paper training, keeping a schedule and crate training.

Paper training details

We could probably call this the old fashion way to housebreak a dog and everyone would know what we are talking about. Long before crates and other methods became popular, everyone use to housebreak a puppy using newspaper.

This method of training is also useful if the weather conditions are difficult or you have a disability that makes it difficult to fuss with a crate or running the puppy outside regularly.

Here is how this method works:

➦ Select the spot you want to use for paper training. Make sure it is not carpeted but has a hard, easy to clean surface. Laundry rooms and little used guest bathrooms are popular choices.

➤ Cover a small area with newspaper. Make the area inviting by placing a toy near the area as well as the food and water bowls. You want the area to invite your puppy to use the space.

➤ Put your dog on the area after eating, sleeping, and playing. These are the most common times that your dog will need to eliminate. If you see your dog squatting or beginning to "go" anywhere else in the house quickly rush him to the paper and place him there until he "goes".

➤ Once your puppy is accustomed to this method, begin to make the paper area smaller and smaller until it is quite small. You can reduce it in small increments either each day or every few days, which ever works best for you and your dog.

➤ When your dog is fully trained to go on the paper, move it outside and encourage your dog to transfer his new potty skill to the outside paper. Eventually, you will be able to get rid of the paper all together and your dog will ask to go outside to eliminate.

There are some advantages to paper training, which include:

➤ This method is particularly convenient for people that live in colder climates and are training their dogs during the winter season. By the time the dog is well trained, moving him to the outdoors should be very easy.

➤ If you have a large house, this method may be easier than trying to quickly get the dog out of doors in time. This is especially true if you have more than one paper area in the house.

➤ Children can easily participate in paper training by learning how to get the dog to the paper in time or putting the dog on the paper after eating or waking from a nap.

➤ This method is easy to use for those that are disabled or older.

Now that we covered the advantages, let's talk about the disadvantages. These include:

➤ Many dogs may have a difficult time making the transition from inside to outside. For some, it is inside or nothing and getting the dog fully trained is a long and difficult process.

➤ Some dogs will not "go" only on the paper, but anywhere in the house because you are essentially training the dog to think it is ok to "go" in the house.

➤ There is maintenance involved in paper training. You must constantly change the papers and keep the area around the paper clean. Depending on your floors, there could be damage.

If you choose to use this method you may want to consider using puppy papers/pads that are designed for this purpose (they absorb moisture better) and are disposable. You can purchase them at many pet supply stores.

Keeping a schedule

Like all babies, a puppy should be on a schedule, though not so firm that you don't allow for the puppy to be a puppy. If you use a schedule and stick to it, housetraining should be fairly easy.

To use the schedule system, simply keep your dog on a regular schedule for feeding, playing, sleeping and eliminating.

When using a schedule, you should always take your dog outside first thing in the morning, after eating, playing and sleeping. In fact these are the times your dog will need to "go" the most.

To make a schedule work, you should feed your dog at the same time every day such as 8 a.m., noon, and 5 p.m. That helps him and you know when it is time to go out (right after eating) and it keeps his little system regular.

This does take some diligence, but you are teaching your puppy to go out after eating, after getting up from a nap and after playing. It is really nothing more than conditioning and that is one of the best ways to train a dog to do anything.

Crate training details

Today, crate training is the method of choice for most dog owners. This is likely due to ease and the melding of the two methods we just talked about, paper training and elements of keeping a schedule.

Here is how it works:

- Get a crate that is just larger than your dog. It is very easy to want a larger crate for comfort but if the crate is too big the puppy will likely soil it. Dogs will not soil in places they have to sleep or eat, so if you keep the crate just large enough to turn around and lay down, you are creating a space that will discourage soiling.

- By the way, choose a crate for the size of your adult dog not the size of your puppy now. If you have to, block off part of the crate so your puppy uses only the part that is big enough for him to turn around and lay down.

- Make the crate comfortable with bedding, food, water bowls and a few toys.

- Take your puppy out of the crate after every nap and meal. That is when he will have to eliminate. Then actively play with him before placing him back in the crate.

- Dogs are den creatures by nature so they enjoy the environment of the crate and will work to keep their den clean. The only time they will eliminate in it is if they are not allowed out often enough to "take care of business."

Eventually, you will be able to keep the door ajar and your dog will retreat into the crate for some quiet time or a snack.

The crate is the dog's safe place, his special place. Do not let children play in the crate!

When using a crate there are some precautions to consider:

➤ First, do not leave your puppy in the crate for long periods of time. This can create numerous behavioral and other type of issues. It will be difficult to housebreak your dog if he is feeling abandoned and neurotic from spending too much time in the crate.

➤ You should never leave your puppy in the crate all day while you are at work. If possible have someone come in at lunch-time and let the dog out, play a little bit and reconnect with the pup.

➤ Make sure the crate is the right size for your dog. Don't take a freebie offered by a friend or relative unless their dog is the same size as your puppy will be when grown. A Crate that is too large will create more problems than it will solve.

Remember that no method will be fully effective unless you apply the principles properly and are committed to the task. Again, we stress that patience and consistency are key to success. Your dog will feed off your energy and will want to please you by doing as you asked.

Housebreaking the rescue or older dog

Housebreaking a dog is a totally different story than housebreaking a puppy. With a puppy, you have a clean slate. They have no expectations or habits to bring to the table.

Your dog has baggage. If you get a dog that is older than a year old (or even 6 months old) who is not yet house broken, he probably has a lot of baggage. You will have your work cut out for you!

You CAN teach your old dog new tricks. Your dog can be taught how to go outside and it can be accomplished fairly quickly. There are, however, some qualities that you must have in order to train your dog to do his business outside.

- Patience
- Consistency
- A knowledge of your dog's personality
- A willingness to change course and do something different if your first effort is not working.
- And did we mention patience?

Before training your dog, be sure you have him checked by your vet to verify there are no medical reasons for accidents.

Also, get as much information as possible about the dog. If you get him from a private party ask if he is house trained and any habits he may have. It could be that his previous owners never had time for him or the dog was left outside much of the time and never learned that it is important to go to the bathroom outside.

If your dog comes from a shelter or rescue do not trust the assessment that the dog is housebroken. Many times they will not have enough time to spend with the animals to really know if they are housebroken. You will just have to find out for yourself when you get your new dog home.

The most likely scenario when you acquire a dog from a shelter, rescue or private party is that the dog is partly housebroken.

Confinement

This method works very well for many dog owners. It is very similar to using a crate, but in this case you use a room or a space for the confinement area.

You can certainly use a crate but if you have a dog that has never been crate trained this could create yet another job for you, teaching your dog how to go into the crate. We suggest that you make working on the house breaking a priority and then if you want to get the dog to use a crate, work on that later.

The best set up for the confinement is a room that has a doggie door to the outside. That way the dog can take himself outside when he needs to go to the bathroom. If a doggie door is not possible, then you must be willing and aware to take the dog out on a regular basis.

When your dog is ready for a nap, take him into his room. Make sure that his space is comfortable and inviting. It should include a bed, some toys and even some food. When he wakes up from his nap, encourage him to go outside through the doggie door if available or by you taking him outside. Make sure your dog being conditioned to go to the bathroom after each nap and sleep. It is also important to take your dog out after meals and playtime.

To summarize, remember it is important to be consistent and patient. Take your dog out after each nap, meal or playtime. If you are kind, but firm with your voice your dog will learn quickly that it is important that he goes outside to the bathroom and that when he does, you are very happy!

Setting a tone

Keep the dog's attention on what is right and what you want him to do. Praise him/her when there is a positive behavior. Always be consistent with your marker: "Yes, good boy/girl." Many dogs that have had no training will quickly figure out what you want and what you are trying to teach them.

When you see your dog squat or act as if he is looking for a place to go, run him outside. You can do this with a firm voice and a word like "outside." Find a phrase that you can use over and over again. Your dog will eventually get the idea that when you say "outside" he is to go to the door and head outside.

If you find that your dog had an accident, and you missed it, point to the mess and go "outside." Make the phrase consistent and take your dog outside. It is not so much as a punishment as a reminder that his business needs to be taken care of outside.

Try to avoid the "rub his nose in it" method of training. This is nothing more than punitive punishment and many dog trainers and experts believe it does little to train a dog. All it does is serve to make him afraid of you and that serves no purpose when it comes to training.

Any method of housebreaking will work on a full grown dog, just pick a method and stick to it!

STEP 12:

Chewing, Biting, and Nipping

Chewing

Chewing is a natural behavior for dogs and helps to promote healthy teeth, gums and jaw muscles. However, there is a downside to chewing. Sometimes a dog may chew some objects that are considered off-limits. This destructive chewing behavior can be caused by many things.

Chewing is also the dog's way of exploring the world around it. Puppies will explore and learn about new things by putting the item in its mouths. This type of exploration can be troublesome as puppies may chew on things that it is not supposed to. Typically young dogs may have great fun chewing on shoes, laces, paper towels and other household items.

When puppies start teething it can lead to a great deal of discomfort. Chewing eases the irritation caused by the growing teeth and they will look for something to relieve themselves of the discomfort. Teething in puppies typically occurs when they are between 3 and 10 months of age.

Like puppies, adult dogs also chew for comfort. They like to put just about anything in their mouths when they are out and about. Especially if what they find is edible.

Chewing gets the puppy in trouble when they aren't provided with legitimate chewing opportunities and forbidden objects are left within reach. Puppy chewing can break teeth, result in swallowed objects, or if chewing an electrical cord a burn. Teething increases the urge to gnaw because it relieves sore gums, but dogs usually continue the habit into adulthood.

Don't try to stop it. Instead, prevent puppy chewing problems by removing temptation, and offering lots of better opportunities.

Puppy chewing

* **Take responsibility for your belongings:** If you don't want it in your dog's mouth, don't make it available. Keep clothing, shoes, books, trash, eyeglasses, your child's stuffed toy, and remote control devices out of your dog's reach.

* **Confine the pup:** When you can't supervise, confine him in a "safe" room or crate with no dangerous or forbidden items. A baby gate works well to control puppy access, and can block off a hallway, stairs, or room.

* **Use repellants:** Make items unpleasant to your dog. Furniture and other items can be coated with a taste deterrent (such as Bitter Apple®) to make them unappealing. Supervise your dog when you first try one of these deterrents. Some dogs will chew an object even if it's coated with a taste deterrent. Also be aware that you must reapply some of these deterrents to maintain their effectiveness.

* **Don't confuse him:** Puppies can't always tell the difference between your new shoes and the old slipper you let him play with. It's best to offer chew toys that he won't confuse with objects you do not want him to have.

* **Make a trade**: Chasing after your puppy to retrieve your shoe becomes a great game of keep-away, and can teach your

puppy to steal things to invite a game of tag. Instead, when you catch your puppy in the act chewing a forbidden object, call the dog's name and redirect the puppy's attention to a legal chew toy as a trade.

➤ **Rotate toys:** Puppies get bored with the same-old every day. Provide at least three to five "legal" options for your chew-happy baby and rotate a couple of times a week. That keeps puppy happy, your precious belongings undamaged, and your fur-kid safe despite himself.

Boredom

A dog may get bored if left alone for extended periods of time and does not have an outlet for his energy. This is especially true for herding and sporting breeds as these tend to need more exercise in order to stay happy.

Help your dog from becoming bored by going for a walk, or you can play a game of fetch. While walking your dog remember to allow time for sniffing and exploration. Walks are also an excellent time to work on a few commands and give praise for a job well done.

You can also take the dog to a park where it can meet other dogs. Socializing with other dogs will help expend a lot of stored up energy. If you do not have enough time to take care of your dog's needs for exercise, you may want to consider hiring a dog walker to help you out for a while.

Separation anxiety

Separation anxiety can also lead to destructive behavior and chewing. Signs of separation anxiety include an overly strong attachment to you. The dog may follow you around even if you are just moving from one room to the next. Your dog may also get anxious when you prepare to leave the house.

Anxiety can occur for several reasons. If you have recently moved, it will take a while for the dog to get used to the its new home. If your schedule changes, it may upset the dog's daily rhythm and it will feel insecure. Anxiety can also occur after the loss of a family member, another household pet or after a stay at a kennel. Dogs who have lived in shelters may also be prone to separation anxiety.

Treating separation anxiety is not easy. But it can be done. One approach involves leaving for short periods of time. Then gradually increase the time it is left alone as it gets used to you being gone. Start out by leaving the dog alone for just a couple of minutes. Then gradually increase it over time until the dog is comfortable being left alone for an hour or two. When treating an anxious dog in this way it is also important that departures and arrivals are made as uneventful as possible.

Other treatments include anti-anxiety medication. This however can usually not be relied upon as a long term solution.

How can I stop my dogs destructive chewing habits?

If your dog engages in destructive chewing behavior, do not yell, scold or punish him unless you actually catch him in the act. Unlike humans, dogs are not able to connect punishment or scolding with an event that occurred an hour ago. It may look like he understands by displaying a submissive behavior or running away. This however is more of a reaction to your tone of voice rather than a reaction to having done something wrong.

You should instead promote non-destructive chewing by way of promoting good behavior, proper socialization, exercise, chew toys, petting and play time.

Mouthing

Puppies like babies explore their world by using their mouth. Puppies learn from their mother and litter mates how much pressure to apply by the reactions that are given. When puppies are playing, they will chew ears, paws, nose, any body part and they learn to gauge what is too hard by a yelp from the one being bitten. This teaches the biting puppy that when he bites too hard the play will end. Through theses play sessions, the puppy will learn bite inhibition and that is why it is very important that puppies stay with their mothers and littermates for at least 8 weeks.

If a dog is removed from the litter before 6 weeks of age he will tend to display more dog mouthing issues during the first period of his life and in some cases, it will continue beyond that. The reason for this is that the dog has been removed from his littermates and his mother just before the first biting and mouthing experiences are properly shaped. The environment in which the puppies have grown up in during their first few weeks also plays an important role, as well as the structure of the litter and other adult dogs in the area.

Once a puppy changes the environment and you bring him into your home, he will try to communicate the only way he knows how, which is by using his mouth. This is also the stage of his dog life when he is developing his instincts, drives and muscular/bone structure as well as his overall coordination. Canine mouthing and chewing behavior seems to be most intense between the ages of three and seven months. Puppies in this stage of development experience discomfort because of teething and are motivated to chew on objects to ease pain caused by their adult teeth coming in. Additionally, puppy mouthing during play very likely serves the important purpose of learning bite inhibition, the ability to control jaw pressure in certain social situations.

Puppies mouth, bite and chew on their owners, just like they do when playing with other dogs. However, despite the fact that puppy mouthing is a completely acceptable behavior when directed at other dogs, most owners find their puppies' play biting painful and unpleasant. The most effective way to deal with this unwanted behavior is not to attempt to eliminate it altogether, but to channel it in the right direction.

A dog uses his jaw and teeth for more complex actions than just eating and biting. It is the dog's only extremity that serves a multiple purpose, from the primary one such as feeding to others such as exploring the environment and physical displays of complex and various social behaviors.

Dog mouthing behaviors start in the earliest stages of a dog's life and although many people think that this kind of "habit" is only displayed while dogs are in their puppyhood, the truth is that dogs are mouthing throughout their entire lives.

DOG MOUTHING ISSUES IN ADULT DOGS

Even though nipping during the early developmental stages of any dog is normal, mouthing in adult dogs is a serious issue that can be dangerous. The problem lays in the fact that as a puppy, this dog grew up in an environment and with situations that didn't properly shape his behavior and in which he wasn't properly addressed for this behavior or perhaps he was encouraged by rewards (this is a type of reward that includes; going out, asking for attention, wanting to play, etc. For example, if your dog is bored and he knows that certain actions, including biting at you, will initiate play with you, he will use this.)

Adult dog mouthing is generally a form of attention seeking behavior which means that at some point the dog learned that he can control the environment and people's reactions by this action. This can be very dangerous because dogs tend to increase pressure in order to get what they want, so in some cases this can turn into an actual bite.

IS THIS BEHAVIOR AGGRESSIVE?

Normally puppies don't display aggressive patterns during early puppyhood, but as the puppy grows older you may see in many cases a switch during their interaction with humans, in which the dog displays a combination of playful and aggressive signals. This can be dangerous as these types of switches are a result of the response that the dog is receiving from the person that he is interacting with.

This is often the reason that dogs tend to be rougher with some family members, than with others.

HOW TO MANAGE THIS BEHAVIOR

There are several different techniques that can be used to address dog mouthing problems, but remember the "safety first" rule. If you are not sure of how to read your dog's signals properly or if you are not sure of what to do, it is always best to contact a professional for assistance.

First of all, dogs won't grow out of this behavior. This is not just a part of puppyhood; it is a rather normal dog behavior.

The best time in a dog's life to address any potential issues on the subject of dog mouthing, is as early as possible.

TRAINING TECHNIQUES FOR DEALING WITH MOUTHING

Control the environment: If the dog is exposed to the environment that encourages his chasing-biting behavior, than your dog will develop stronger reactions to movement and will often react with his mouth.

Teasing your dog with your hands (rapidly moving your hands) will only encourage him to persist and want to grab your hands even more.

Respond to the behavior: Dogs in the early stages of their lives are easily influenced. You can use this to your advantage. There are a few simple things that you can do when your puppy starts nipping. If the game becomes too rough, simply "yelp" and stop playing. Stop all activities and ignore your puppy for a few seconds, then engage the game again. This is important, as just yelping alone and continuing play will only intrigue your puppy even more, the game has to stop at that moment, and cannot resume until the dog's behavior is acceptable (he calms down).

It is very important to restart the game. The purpose of this break wasn't to punish your dog, but to deliver feedback to him. Giving a response and feedback during the interaction with your dog is crucial for his development. This is the way he learns to adjust his game and the strength of his approach.

Ignoring the behavior: This is probably one of the best techniques to use, although it is usually the hardest. Young dogs will often try to engage a playing session by grabbing/biting at your legs, hands, clothes, etc. How you react, will mold your dog's behavior patterns. Responding to your dog's signals (in this case, the mouthing), will teach your dog that his actions create response, and he will begin using this "technique" whenever he wants to activate you. This is the road to attention seeking behavior issues.

If your dog realizes that he can make you move and play, simply by practicing the mouthing behavior, he will increase that behavior and you will face a long, difficult, and time-consuming retraining period to resolve this issue.

Example: If you are in position where your dog is mouthing your hand while you are sitting to get you to play with him even if you would like to do so, you don't want to reward his behavior. This will encourage the bad behavior in the future. Instead, do a simple redirecting technique. Don't move your body. Wait for the second that he stops mouthing; as soon as he stops, start playing.

Whatever you do, be sure to allow a few seconds between the dog's mouthing and actually playing with him or performing other interactions. These few seconds should be enough for your dog to not connect his mouthing with your response, as a form of reward.

Redirecting dog mouthing: As mentioned earlier, dog mouthing is a normal behavior and activity, our goal is to lower this behavior to a minimum and redirect it to different objects in the environment, like toys.

Every time a dog gets into a mouthing pattern, redirect him to a toy or a chew bone. Be careful when using this method that you redirect in a way that is not rewarding.

It is not advisable to use your body as a toy. If you do, your dog will not understand why he cannot mouth you (for example, playing with your hands or feet, encouraging him to chase or bite at you). Instead, always redirect him to, or play with, a toy that he can focus his mouth on.

Once your dog is ready, simply start marking and rewarding the behaviors in which he is calm around your hands or other body parts (for example, mark the moment that your dog releases your hands and then redirect him with treats so that he does not associate the mouthing, but instead the act of "not-mouthing" with the reward, etc.).

Remember, that it is important to train alternate behavior responses. Many people make the mistake of putting all of their focus on how to stop an issue, without training an alternate behavior like sits or down, to the dog. This is just important as dealing with the issue itself. If you are trying to change or extinguish a certain behavior without offering a substitute action, this may end up being a frustrating and impossible task simply because a dog won't know what else to do instead.

Why dogs bite

Every dog has the potential to bite. Luckily for us, most don't. Dogs don't "bite without warning." They bite when their warning signals go unheeded. It is often not a single trigger, but an accumulation of triggers in a designated time period without relief which cause the bite event.

Many times, pet owners don't recognize the warning signs before a bite, so they think their dogs are suddenly flying off the handle and going crazy. However, that's rarely the case. It can be just a nano second between a warning and a bite, but again, dogs rarely bite without giving some type of warning beforehand.

WARNING SIGNS A DOG WILL BITE:

➤ **Growling and snapping** are probably the most obvious signs that a dog is about to bite. Dogs growl to let you know they are unhappy. If a dog growls at you when you approach, it's time to give him some space. Knowing what causes the growling allows you to manage the problem and work on changing the behavior.

➤ **Wagging the tail:** A dog who is about to bite is usually fairly rigid, and his tail will be pointed high and moving more quickly back and forth. This may be a sign that your dog is going to bite.

➤ **Raised fur:** When dogs are afraid, you may see the hair on their backs stand up.

➤ **Rigid body posture:** The dog's entire body may go stiff, and his ears and tail are raised high. If you reach out to pet a dog, and his entire body freezes rather than wiggling to get closer, he is not happy with being touched.

➤ **Licking his lips (when food is not involved), yawning repeatedly, or turning his head to avoid meeting your gaze, he is trying to tell you something.** Dogs show these behaviors to let you know they are uncomfortable with something going on around them. For instance, a dog who has never been around children may lick his lips or yawn when a child comes over to pet him. It does not necessarily mean that he is about to bite, but it is a warning that he is not comfortable. A dog that is uncomfortable, afraid, or stressed is more likely to bite. Your best bet when a dog uses one of these appeasement gestures is to try to alleviate his discomfort.

➤ **Cowering and tail tucking:** Cowering and tail tucking are more overt signs than lip licking or yawning that you are dealing with a fearful dog. While fearful dogs don't always bite, fear does increase the likelihood. If you encounter a dog who cowers away from you with his tail tucked between his legs, back off. Let him approach you in his own time, and he'll be less likely to feel the need to bite

→ **Seeing the whites of the eyes:** Many dog trainers refer to this as whale eye. You'll see the whites of a dog's eye when he moves his head slightly, but doesn't move his eyes. A half moon of white will show around the dog's eyes. Whale eye is a sign of anxiety in dogs. This doesn't necessarily mean that a dog is about to bite. It means that a dog is feeling anxious, and anxious dogs are more likely to bite. If you see a dog showing the whites of his eyes, it's a good idea to give him some space until he feels more relaxed.

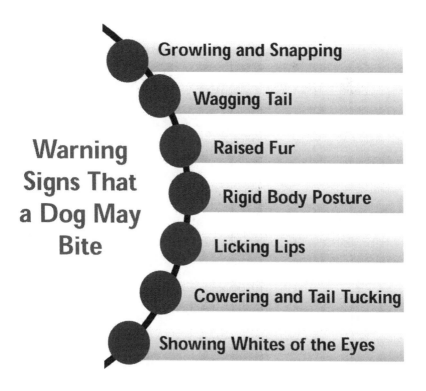

Warning Signs That a Dog May Bite

- Growling and Snapping
- Wagging Tail
- Raised Fur
- Rigid Body Posture
- Licking Lips
- Cowering and Tail Tucking
- Showing Whites of the Eyes

HERE ARE A FEW REASONS WHY DOGS BITE:

→ **Fear aggression**: Like people, dogs are naturally fearful of unfamiliar and potentially threatening situations. These dogs are very uncertain and tentative in their actions. When they are faced with new situations, people, or dogs they avoid direct eye contact and assume a low submissive stance. They stand with their ears flat against their heads and their tails tucked between their legs. They bend their head and neck toward any individual that seeks their attention while they lick their lips. They will often roll on their backs exposing their belly. Their expression is one of profound worry. They are very fearful about being touched and shy away from being petted stroked or brushed. At any instant they may snap and bite in fear. Fearfully aggressive dogs often bite from behind when the interaction is ending. These dogs often back up immediately after they have been aggressive.

→ **Dominance aggression**: In cases of dogs who bite due to dominance aggression, it is usually members of the dog's human family that are most often the victims. They may innocently attempt to move a dog off the sofa; push down on his rump to have him sit, step over a dog who's laying inconveniently in the doorway and the dog erupts in a "you'd better not do that" vocal warning, followed by a bite. In each situation, the dog believes that he is in charge and that his humans have not earned the status to tell him what to do. This potentially dangerous behavior disorder is rooted in a struggle for control.

→ **Protection of valuables**: Some dogs believe the only way to protect their valuables is through an act of aggression. A dog's list of valuables may include food, toys, territory (a house or a car) or even their human family members. Possessive aggressive behavior is a learned reaction to having a favorite valuable, food or bed taken away and not replaced. It is also a means of controlling the environment. This behavior is very common in dogs that have been abandoned, lost or allowed to control the household.

➔ **Redirected aggression**: An attempt to break up a dog fight is the most common scenario for this category of biting. Two dogs are barking, posturing and biting at each other when all of a sudden hands reach in and grab at collars, tails and hind legs. The excited dogs blindly whip around and land bites to body parts of the interrupters.

➔ **Pain-induced aggression**: Any dog may bite if hurting, depending on the degree of pain. An otherwise gentle dog will bite an owner's hand trying to soothe, bandage or examine wounds. Like us, each dog has a unique pain threshold and tolerance

➔ **Maternal aggression:** The first two to three weeks after a female dog gives birth, her puppies rely on her for all they need to survive: warmth, nutrition, stimulation to prompt elimination and protection. Even the most outgoing, well-trained dog may show signs of maternal aggression if she feels her newborns are at risk.

➔ **Provocation**: Unfortunately, many people just don't know how to treat dogs. It's hard to blame a dog for biting if the dog is being poked with a stick, jumped on, or having its tail pulled.

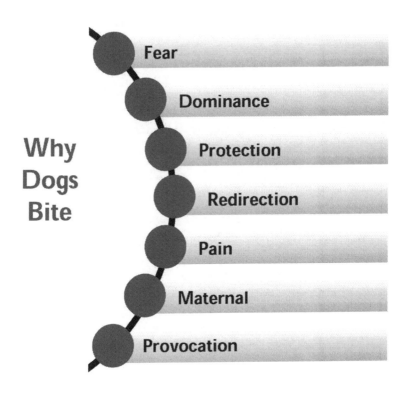

Why Dogs Bite

Fear

Dominance

Protection

Redirection

Pain

Maternal

Provocation

STEP 13:

Jumping

Puppies and dogs will naturally jump up on people when they want to say hello. Why? Because we're taller than they are! When dogs meet, they sniff each other's faces. They like to do the same thing when greeting us, so it's perfectly natural for dogs to jump up on us to try to reach our faces and get our attention.

When your dog jumps on you, the goal is to get your attention and to get you to pet or play with him.

Knowing this, you can show your dog what is needed to earn your attention and touch.

Try to remember two things each time you greet your dog:

1. Keep your attention and your hands away from your dog unless her front feet are on the floor. Put your hands in your pocket or let them hang by your side but do not touch your dog

2. Immediately give your dog attention and petting the instant her front feet land on the floor in a sit or stand position.

When you enter a door and your dog jumps up on you, ignore the dog. Don't yell to get off and don't push away. Instead, stand up straight and look over the dogs head. If the jumping continues, turn away. Your dog will have to put their front paws on the floor to follow you. The instant their front paws touch the floor, mark with a "YES, GOOD GIRL/BOY"! If your dog jumps up at your touch, just pull your hand away, stand up straight like before, and ignore until the paws find the floor again. The moment her feet touch the floor, mark with the word "yes" and pet your dog. Your attention and your touch are the words that will show your dog how she needs to act to get your attention.

Never withhold attention to your dog when your dog's feet finally do touch the floor-even if you're irritated for jumping a moment earlier. Your dog has to be able to make the connection that front feet on the floor magically result in attention and affection from you and other people.

Jumping solutions

➔ Avert your eyes and turn sideways when your dog is about to jump, this will deflect the dog and once your dog has all 4 paws on the ground, wait for a few seconds and then pet or give affection.

➔ Another option is to walk into the dog when the dog jumps. By walking into the dog you invade their space and they will not be able to stay on 2 legs. Once all 4 paws are on the ground, give your attention.

STEP 14:

Barking

Barking is a dog's way to communicate. They are not meant to be silent and were given their voices for a reason- to protect, to communicate and to be heard. But, some dogs and humans, too, just can't be quiet. They continue barking long after the UPS truck has left the street and react vocally to just about any sound, any movement in their backyards or homes.

These are the dogs that may suffer from chronic barking disease and these are the dogs that can make you crazy. Many of these dogs can't control themselves, working themselves into a frenzy as they bark at whatever moves them, literally and figuratively.

If you are desperate to learn how to quiet these barky pups, to get them to learn how to bark only when necessary and appropriate, boy, do we have ideas for you! That is what this chapter is all about, dealing with your chronic barker.

It is likely that while you may be tired of your dogs incessant barking, you also do not want to fully quiet him. You want your dog to warn and protect you and your house. To warn you when you need to be warned and maybe even have a voice during playtime. However, you need your dog to understand limits, and you have come to the right place.

Why do dogs bark?

At first glance, this may seem like a silly question. Clearly it is a form of communication but it is a bit more complicated than that.

Dogs bark for any number of reasons, as many reasons as we speak, cough, and laugh. Dogs want to communicate but they may also have deeper reasons.

FUN

Many dogs bark quite simply because it is fun. Like people, many dogs like the sound of their own voice and want to hear it as much as possible. They might get a reaction from other pets or other dogs in the area. Even YOU may provide a reaction they like!

When dogs are at play they may bark or yelp in order to communicate that they are having fun, want to play more and are enjoying themselves. Sometimes they bark because they are afraid of the dog they are playing with, or your play has become too scary or overwhelming for them.

SOME REASONS THAT DOGS BARK INCLUDE:

WARNING/ALERT

FUN

ATTENTION

EXCITEMENT

PLAYFULNESS

ANXIETY/SEPARATION ATTENTION

BOREDOM

OTHER DOGS

SOCIAL BARKING

Types of barks

Most barks send a clear message and knowing what your dog is saying is critical to understanding why he is barking.

ALERT

Barking that indicates a dog is alert will be **continuous and fast**. It may not be necessarily loud, (and yes there are different volumes of voice your dog can use), but it will convey a message that your dog is alert and wants you to know something. It may mean that someone has entered the yard, home or territory.

DEFENSE MODE

If your dog is barking continuously but **slowly and the bark is heard at low volume**, the dog is preparing to defend himself. To the dog, the intruder (or his perception of the intruder) is near. If this is what you are hearing you should likely have the understanding that the dog is scared but ready to protect if necessary.

LONELY

Think your dog might be lonely? If so you may have heard a bark that features a **high pitched** voice and the barks are **long and drawn out**. There will be pauses between the barks. That is a bark that lets you know your dog is lonely and wants your company. This may be the bark he uses when you are not home and drives your neighbors crazy!

TROUBLE APPROACHING

A **fast** bark that also features **pauses with every third or fourth bark** is a dog's way of saying he thinks trouble is approaching. Instead of taking matters in to his own paws or voice, he is asking for a response from you.

HAPPY

A **short** bark that is **neither too loud nor soft** is letting you know he is happy. He is curious and alert (but not stressed) if you hear a single bark greeting. This is normal.

REALLY HAPPY!

Your dog will likely greet you or friends on a normal basis with a **high-pitched** bark that features **one or two short barks**. This is the "I am really happy to see you" bark.

SURPRISED

Is your dog surprised? You will likely hear a bark that is **short and high pitched**. If this bark is repeated, your dog is trying to get you to look at something or get your attention.

PAIN

A **single yelp** or **very short high-pitched** bark means, "Ouch!" This is in response to a sudden, unexpected pain.

SEVERE FEAR AND/OR PAIN

Series of yelps: "I'm hurting!" "I'm really scared" This is in response to severe fear and pain.

There are many different types of barks you can listen for, but the end result is this—dogs bark and they bark for specific reasons. They want to communicate and want to be heard. Their bark is their voice.

The problems begin when your dog barks and continues to bark after the message has been sent, the issue has been resolved, or for no reason at all. That is when the neighbors, the dog owner and others become stressed or unhappy.

Let's take a look at chronic barking!

Chronic barking

Knowing what constitutes chronic barking is important, but it is equally important to know if your dog really has a problem or if he is within the realm of normal.

All dogs bark, so it is hard to determine which type of barking is normal or chronic. You may think your dog barks too much but his barking may be completely normal for his breed or personality. By contrast, you may think your dog is a non-barker but your neighbors disagree.

YOUR PERCEPTIONS

Perceptions are important with regard to your dog barking, especially your perception. Your dog might not be a chronic barker at all but your perception may be that he barks too much.

Many people feel that dogs are like children, they should be seen and not heard but that is not very realistic. Dogs use their voice to communicate so some barking should be expected, normal and acceptable. Barking can in fact provide a real benefit to you and others as dogs can save lives through their appropriate and focused barking.

So, consider your own ideas about what you consider appropriate barking, your reactions to your dog's barking and whether the barking is in reality appropriate. If you can look at the situation objectively, and you think your dog may be a chronic barker then read on!

BREEDS TO CONSIDER

When considering the root cause of barking, it is important to consider the previously mentioned reasons, but also take into account the breed of the dog. Some breeds are simply prone to bark more than others. The following breeds are considered to be more "barky" than others.

+ Maltese
+ Shih Tzu
+ Bassett Hound
+ Australian Cattle Dog

➼ English Springer Spaniel
➼ Pomeranian
➼ Bull Mastiff
➼ Rottweiler
➼ Fox Terrier
➼ Beagle

Now, just because you may have one of these breeds (or a mixed breed of one of the listed dogs) does not mean your dog will bark incessantly, just be aware they may have a tendency to bark more.

There are also a few dogs that are much less likely to bark. These include:
➼ Golden Retriever
➼ Akita
➼ Bloodhound
➼ Labrador Retriever
➼ Great Dane
➼ Newfoundland

WHAT DOG BREEDS DON'T BARK

Some dogs are physically unable to bark, while others bark very rarely. Keep in mind that although they may not be able to or chose not to bark very much. They still make other noises and vocalizations in order to communicate. Some of these dogs include:
➼ Shiba Inu
➼ Basenji

Of course, you must also consider your dog's personality. There may be some Golden Retrievers that bark with the best of them and some Maltese that rarely make a peep. The important thing to understand is your dog's personality and basic tendency so you can allow a bit of barking if your dog is from a breed prone to bark or not be surprised if your less barking breed decides to be a barker.

IS YOUR DOG A CHRONIC BARKER?

What constitutes chronic barking? Let's look at a few scenarios and see what YOU think!

➤ **Max** is a mixed breed adult dog. He is inside most of the time but enjoys going outside to run around and bask in the sunshine and sniff the dog next door. When Max hears a noise, any noise, he is on it! He barks until he no longer hears the sound.

Often Max will bark at the neighbor next door when she brings in her garbage cans each week at the same time like clockwork. Max will bark with abandon each time from the moment she starts making noise until a few minutes after she goes back inside. **Is Max a chronic barker?**

➤ **Princess** is a two year old Pomeranian that rarely goes outside, but to take care of business. She believes her territory is inside and spends most of her time in the front room sleeping or looking out the window.

Princess barks quite a bit. She barks when the mail carrier leaves a package at the door and when the children come home from school. She often has to be scolded, but she continues barking as long as she feels the need, which is often. **Is Princess a chronic barker?**

➤ **Charlie** is a large Rottweiler that spends most of his time outside. He digs holes, runs around the yard, and occasionally spends time in his dog run. Even though he is a large dog, he has a low bark, but uses his voice often, many times barking well into the night. Charlie is a friendly dog and when his owners tell him to quiet he often does, but will continue barking as soon as they have gone back into the house.

Is Charlie a chronic barker?

WHO ARE THE CHRONIC BARKERS?

So, are Max, Princess and Charlie chronic barkers?

Max has a barking demeanor that could be described as perfectly normal. He barks when he thinks he needs to respond to something that needs his attention. He also barks out of habit (like the neighbor bringing in the garbage cans). His barking really poses no problems for his family or the neighbors.

Princess is a Pomeranian, and just by the nature of Pomeranians, she will be prone to barking more than some other dogs. Although, her barking may be annoying, it does not seem to be chronic. Of course, it helps that she is indoors much of the time.

Charlie, the Rottweiler, has a bit of a barking problem. He is left outdoors often, is a breed that has a tendency to bark more, and seems to get very little hands on attention or involvement from his owners. Charlie is likely a chronic barker.

CHRONIC BARKING CHECKLIST:

You might see elements of your dog's behavior in each of these dogs and still wonder- is my dog a chronic barker?

Here are several things to consider:

- [✓] Does your dog bark at things or does your dog bark at nothing? Dogs that bark at specific noises tend to be more purposeful and less likely to move into chronic barking. They will bark at the noise or person and then stop when the situation changes.

- [✓] Does your dog bark for long periods of time? Most dogs that are not chronic barkers will bark for a short period of time then stop. If your dog barks for long periods of time, barks at anything and anyone you have a chronic barker. Chronic barkers are not discriminating in their barking.

- [✓] Have you received complaints about your dog barking? Although some people may have unreasonable expectations about a dog's barking or behavior, most people will only complain if the dog is a nuisance. If you have received complaints about your dog, it is important to remember that the complainer felt the need to make a specific complaint about your dog's behavior.

- [✓] Does your dog have any physical ailments that might be caused by chronic barking? Many chronic barkers will have some health problems associated with stress, like ulcers or immune system damage.

Many dogs will bark and many more will chronically bark. Solving the problem is not as easy as telling them to be quiet. The issues go deeper than that. Let's explore some of those reasons- Read on!

Dogs are funny and interesting creatures. They can be difficult to figure out, because there are many things that motivate them, challenge them and so many expectations they have for us. Yes, your dog does have expectations for you.

Chronic barking may be a combination of factors. It could be bad behavior on the part of your dog, or it may be part of a behavior that you inadvertently rewarded or played a part in. Whatever the case, it is important to realize the root cause of the bark fest.

If you use some of the intervention methods we will be discussing later, but do not change the core issue it is likely that the barking or other misbehavior will again become a focus.

There are times that we as dog owners unwittingly cause or aggravate a problem, and that leaves us to fix it.

Let's look at the myriad of reasons that a dog can get into a cycle of chronic barking.

FRUSTRATION

Yes, dogs like people get frustrated. A dog that has had a change in any area of his life may not be happy. In order to express frustration, your dog will bark (because barking is a form of communication) to get your attention and let you know how unhappy he may be, so you can change the situation.

To determine if frustration is why your dog is barking, ask yourself a few questions. Did you move? Did someone move in or out? Is he spending more time inside or outside? Are you working longer hours? Are you able to play with him as

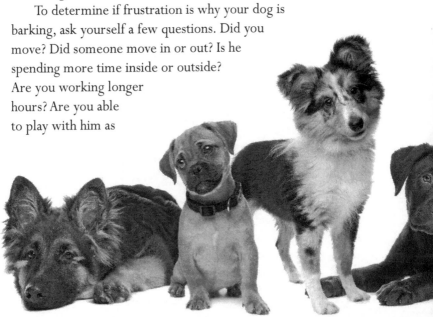

much as you were previously? What changed in the household? What changed with his situation? Consider all possibilities and you may find the root cause of your dog's barking.

BARRIER FRUSTRATION

Barrier frustration is a more specific upset for your dog. Did you install a new fence that limits your dog's movement or line of sight? Are you now keeping him on a leash? Did you just begin crate training or install a new dog run?

BREED

We briefly discussed breed, but again, you must think about breed when considering why your dog barks too much. If your dog is a breed known for barking there is only so much you can do to control the barking, but there are some intervention measures that can be used effectively to reduce the amount of barking.

STRESS

Stress and frustration can be closely linked. Dogs feel stress like we do. Many dogs do not accept change, just like some people do not accept change. Is your dog barking because he is stressed? Consider the following:

➤ Is there a new baby or household member?

➤ Is there a new pet?

➤ Is there a health issue? Either yours or your dog? Dogs know when we do not feel well and many times they want to help us feel better.

➤ Did you move to a new house or have new surroundings?

➤ Are you under a lot of stress due to your work or other issues?

➤ Did your neighbor get a new puppy or dog?

LONELINESS

Dogs are social animals that need to be around other animals and people. Your dog might be lonely because you are gone much of the time or because he needs a friend.

Take a moment to think about your dog's temperament. While dogs by nature are social animals, not all dogs need to be social all the time. Is your dog friendly and love to see other dogs and people? If so, does he get that opportunity often? If you think your dog may be lonely, consider making a plan that you can enact to help your dog feel social and happy. Lonely dogs are destructive dogs and having your dog communicate loneliness by barking could turn into other more destructive behaviors.

EXCITEMENT

Many dogs get excited easily and have a hard time calming down once the initial excitement is over and continue barking because they do not know what to do next. They are excited and want everyone to know what they have seen, heard, and what experiences they have had.

Some dogs are naturally more excitable than others, so think about that when you are considering if your dog is barking out of excitement. Learning how to control your dog or bring him down from his excitement is critical if you want to stop the barking.

LACK OF STIMULATION

The opposite of excitement is lack of stimulation. This can cause your dog to bark to create his own excitement, by barking.

By being bored and restless your dog will bark to send the message, "Hey, I am bored and restless, pay attention to me".

Dogs that are kept outside in the yard for long periods of time, are not taken for walks, given playtime by their owners are likely to begin barking because of a lack of stimulation. They bark because it gives them a stimulation that they do not have in their lives.

DOMINANCE

If a dog perceives there is no leadership in the household, no alpha dog, per se, he will set himself up into the hierarchal position to be the alpha dog. Dogs need to know that someone is in charge in a position of dominance. They do not necessarily want to be the dominant one, and most dogs are very happy to leave that to someone else. If no one steps up and acts like the dominant party in the household, the dog will take that role.

Barking then becomes the dog's way to establish himself as the ruler of the house. He will continue to bark to remind everyone of his position and that he can't be trifled with. You now have to take back your power from your dog in order to stop this type of barking.

NO TRAINING

We do not mean obedience training here. We mean that perhaps your chronic barker might not have been taught that unnecessary barking is not ok. Dogs should learn through feedback we give them, that their bark is a good thing and serves a valuable service. We also need to teach them that when they are finished communicating the message they need to stop making the noise.

If you have never taught your dog that they need to stop barking after communicating the message, or you have "talked" back somehow, you have sent the message that barking is ok, not that barking must cease after a reasonable amount of time.

BARKING HAS BEEN REWARDED

As owners, we sometime unwittingly encourage barking by rewarding our dogs in ways we may not think of as rewards. For example, if the dog is let into the house when it barks, this is providing a consequence, but a consequence that the dog likes. So when the dog wants to come inside, he may bark incessantly until you let him back in the house. The lesson taught is "If I bark, they will let me in the house!" Therefore, barking gets the desired result.

By the same token, if your dog is lonely or has felt ignored and when he barks you yell, that is giving him the attention and a response from you, one which he may not get any other way. This is a hard habit to break, but it can be done and we will talk about breaking a conditioned behavior shortly.

OUTSIDE CONDITIONING

This last reason for chronic barking is a very common problem, perhaps more common than you think. When dogs bark and our neighbors get annoyed, some may try and be nice, and that leads to more barking.

Here is how it works:

Your dog is in the yard and your neighbor decides to work in his garden. Your dog sees the neighbor and begins to bark. Your neighbor begins to talk to your dog in a friendly manner trying to get your dog to stop barking, and it works. Now your neighbor has unwittingly conditioned the behavior.

Your dog will bark each time he sees your neighbor and the chronic barking will become more of a problem as the dog and your neighbor engage in what amounts to a power struggle that has no clear winner and no clear end.

Intervention and resolution

Retraining is about teaching your dog not to bark and about retraining or relearning his habits and impulses. Your dog will always have the impulse to bark but the goal is to stop the chronic and unnecessary barking.

We will examine some retraining methods you can use to quiet your dog. Some can be used alone and others can be combined for a more effective result.

NO BARK COMMAND

This may also be called a quiet command. This command is teaching your dog that it is ok to bark when necessary, but he must learn to control and turn off the bark.

Here is how it works:

Start by getting your dog to bark. You could play with him, have someone go outside and make some noise that will encourage barking. You can also bark at him because dogs like to mimic. Once he is barking, quickly and gently hold his mouth shut and say "quiet" or "quiet now".

This sends the message that it is alright to bark for a period of time but when it is time to be quiet, it is time to stop and be quiet.

Make sure you praise your dog quite a bit for barking and then being asked to be quiet. It is very likely that this will be the first time he has been praised for shutting his mouth.

Next, work on teaching him to be quiet in a real world scenario. The next time he barks at a noise, stranger, or whatever provokes him, praise him for using his voice. You can use the phrase "Good voice" or "good (name)". This lets your dog know that his voice is ok and barking is fine within reason.

Keep your voice excited and be sure to praise your dog lavishly for using his voice. Then follow the praise with a neutral sounding "ok" and then a firm "quiet". Once quiet, praise him again for being quiet using a very excited tone.

The whole sequence will look like this: Your dog barks at some-thing and you say "good Voice" Good (name)", the "ok" and follow with the firm "quiet".

In doing this you are effectively communicating to your dog what you want him to know. That it is ok to bark at strangers or question-able noises, but after providing the alert it is time to stop barking.

Although this method will work better with younger dogs, with patience and consistency you can teach the older dog to fully under-stand the "no bark command".

Remember that the objective here is to teach the dog that it is perfectly fine to alert you to others, intruders, bark in fun or to communicate, but it needs to be to a point and then stop.

IGNORE THE DOG

If it appears that your dog is barking to get attention or to get a reaction from you, this method will give the dog nothing.

For example, if your dog barks to come in, ignore him. He will stop barking but this might take some time (as he is a chronic barker after all) but he will eventually give up and lay down or move on to other pursuits. Once he does quiet down and moves on to other things, you can open the door and let him in. This way, he learns that you are willing to open the door without a big show and noise.

Dogs, being very smart, will no doubt come up with a new way to let you know that he wants to go in the house, like a light scratch on the door.

If you have a neighbor that will talk to your barking dog to try and get him to stop barking (and has unwittingly made the problem worse), ask your neighbor to stop reacting by talking to your dog. Explain that you believe ignoring him when your dog barks will resolve the problem.

This method absolutely takes some patience and consistency. You must be consistent. If you are not consistent than you will confuse your dog and teach him that his action gets the desired reaction from you.

MAKE YOURSELF THE BOSS

Many times, dogs will become chronic barkers because there is no clear power figure in the household. They want a leader. They want someone to establish themselves as a leader. If no one takes the position your dog will step up and claim the position. Then the barking begins.

If you think that the lack of a clear leader in your household has led your dog to become a serious barker, begin to establish yourself as the authority.

Consider your dog's breed and general temperament before you attempt this, so you have a decent idea of how long it will take the dog to come around to your side and how long you can expect to wait before you see the results of your effort.

Finally, think about the many opportunities you have on a daily basis to let your dog know that you are the boss. Perhaps when you get home from work you change your clothes first before greeting your dog, or make him wait outside until you are ready to see him. Thinking about your daily routine should provide many opportunities to place yourself in the boss position.

BREAK CONDITIONING

We all know that dogs are a product of conditioning. Through conditioning is how your dog learns the rules of the house. However, you can break a dog of conditioning by patiently working with your dog. If you unwittingly taught your dog it was ok to bark, you now have to break that bad habit. With some persistence, patience and consistency, it can be done!

Let's say that when your dog was a puppy, he was somewhat reticent to have his voice heard. Someone would come to the door and he would barely make a peep. As he got older and his confidence grew, so did his voice and you rewarded him for that. You were thrilled he was finally using his voice. You both realized that his voice could be useful for different things. Now, he barks when someone gets near the door, the mail carrier, and the neighbors cat. He barks at small birds and animals, grocery bags, and your ringing cell phone. He just won't stop! You now have a monster. Now, if your dog is a chronic barker and has not been conditioned but barks out of habit or fun, perhaps just to hear his voice, have heart, these dogs are easiest to retrain!

How do you break this conditioning? It is simply a matter of re-conditioning. Dogs can learn new tricks and your dog can learn that his barking is problematic for you.

For example, some dog owners find that providing their dog with a treat when not barking works well. Others may use the "ignore" method and work through that for as long as it takes for the dog to be reconditioned.

You may hear other trainers speak about using a spray bottle of water. Blue Line K-9 does not recommend this form of teaching your dog not to bark for the simple reason your dog may become aggressive towards the bottle and will only listen when the bottle is present.

Dogs are pretty quick learners and it should not take long for your dog to figure out that you are sending a message when you issue the command of "no bark " or "quiet" without a spray of water.

If your dog is a water lover, you may as well skip this method because there is a good chance your dog will think you are playing and that defeats your purpose.

GIVE YOUR DOG A TREAT

Yes, that's right, a treat. One method that can be successful in getting your dog to stop barking is to provide him with a treat. Much like teaching the "quiet "command, in this version you get your dog to bark and then give him a treat. DO NOT just hand it to him, but hold on to the treat as he licks it or begins to eat it. Since he is licking or eating the treat he is now unable to bark and you can provide a "good dog" or other positive comment.

This method seems to be especially effective with puppies that will be easily distracted by the treat and are sometimes hard to train because they are so busy.

Depending on which methods you choose to retrain your dog, you can often also use a treat. When your dog behaves in a way that you find acceptable, in this case not barking, provide him with a treat and a very enthusiastic "good boy!" It is not necessary but it makes the job all that much sweeter for your dog.

COMBINE METHODS

Most of these retraining methods can be mixed and matched. You can combine them and find the one that is right for you.

A FEW MORE TIPS

Most dog experts agree that yelling at your dog serves no purpose. It may be that your dog perceives that you are barking back and in that case he will learn nothing.

Focus on your end result-no more chronic barking and keep these tips in mind:

- **Be patient and consistent.** As with children, dogs respond to consistency, so it is best to select a method that you think will work the best and stick with it.

- **Be generous with praise.** Dogs, like people loved to be praised and will respond well to your happy and enthusiastic voice. Providing, praise will go a long way toward breaking the barking habit.

- Chronic barking did not develop over night and breaking the habit will not happen overnight either. It takes time so keep up your efforts and be willing to wait for the results.

- Consider changing the household structure to accommodate your new anti-barking standards. If you need to change how or when your dog comes inside, the people he interacts with or the arrangements for where and how he sleeps during the day, do so. The end result of no barking will be worth it.

DEVOCALIZATION (DEBARKING) AND OTHER METHODS TO QUIET YOUR DOG

It is important to preface this section by saying that the methods that will be discussed are controversial and NOT necessarily supported by Blue Line K-9.

However, we feel that it is important to at least cover the topics and bring up to date information to you, our reader. Please talk to your vet about any methods that require surgery. Your vet may have other suggestions for methods that may work with your dog.

Debarking is a very controversial subject. The term "devocalization" is misleading, because the procedure does not render the animal voiceless or silent. The proper term is ventriculocordectomy. When ventriculocordectomy is correctly performed, there is about a 50 percent reduction in volume and a lower pitch to the bark.

There are two types of ventriculocordectomy procedures: the **laryngotomy technique** and the **oral technique**. The most common procedure is the oral technique. This bark softening procedure is noninvasive and takes one to two minutes to perform, using a very short-acting injectable anesthetic. In this technique, the dog's mouth is opened and a very small piece of tissue is taken from one or both vocal folds, using a slender biopsy instrument. When correctly done, there is little to no bleeding or discomfort. Recovery takes place within a few minutes and the dog is able to eat and drink immediately. There is no change in the dog's behavior or attitude. The dog can and does continue to bark, but the bark is roughly half as loud as it was before the procedure. There is no way to predict or control the volume of the bark and the bark may have a raspy sound. Results vary among dogs and are usually permanent, although in some cases dogs may eventually regain full volume of their bark.

The laryngotomy procedure is more involved and risky. This technique involves making a two-inch incision on the skin of the neck, above the dog's larynx, separating the muscles, cauterizing blood vessels, entering the larynx, removing all of the dog's vocal fold tissue and stitching the incision back together. This technique is invasive, painful, requires anesthesia and has a prolonged recovery time. There can be serious postoperative complications, including scarring formation, delayed healing and tissue damage. Scarring can be so extensive that the dog can have difficulty breathing for the rest of its life.

Bark softening is not a procedure of convenience. It is reserved for severe cases in which behavior modification efforts have failed.

The American Veterinary Medical Association's position on devocalization is: "Canine devocalization should only be performed by qualified, licensed veterinarians as a final alternative after behavioral modification efforts to correct excessive vocalization have failed."

As of this writing, debarking procedure is outlawed as a form of mutilation in the United Kingdom and all countries that have signed the European Convention for the Protection of Pet Animals. So far in the United States, devocalization/debarking is illegal by state law in: Ohio by citation for dogs that have been deemed vicious, the Commonwealth of Massachusetts, state of New Jersey, and by city ordinance in Warwick, Rhode Island. Efforts to ban devocalization are underway in other states.

ANTI-BARKING COLLARS

There are several different types of anti barking collar.

➤ **Citronella collar:** Citronella is a natural lemon-scented spray that dogs don't like. The collar is designed to not-spray in their faces but have it mist up so they smell the lemon. The type of collar delivers a harmless burst of citronella spray that distracts your dog and interrupts your dog's barking. The spray works with four of the dog's five senses - he hears it, sees it, feels it and smells it.

➤ **High-frequency collars:** Make a very high pitched noise that is usually undetectable to humans, but startling and uncomfortable for a dog. The better versions of any of these collars offer the option of a delayed reaction, allowing the dog to bark a few times before triggering.

➤ **Electronic dog collars (shock collars):** The electronic anti-bark dog collar is also called a shock collar for dogs. This is a battery operated device that attaches to a training collar. When a dog begins to bark this device will emit a shock equivalent to a static charge. This negative reinforcement will get the dog's attention and break the cycle of unrelenting barking. After several shocks the dog is going to realize that the barking is what triggers the shock and this will cause him to stop barking so that he can avoid the small jolt of static electricity.

Some final notes on barking...

Hopefully by now you are on the right track and have a good idea of why your dog is barking as well as how to get him to stop being a chronic barker.

Dogs bark for many reasons, including excitement, playfulness, warning, fear, separation anxiety and loneliness. There are many things dog owners can do to prevent barking problems.

First, they should keep in mind the fact that dogs bark and make noise. Dogs want attention. People, who are away from home for long periods of time, or who are too busy to care for a dog and give it the attention it needs, shouldn't have a dog. Next, people should always do their homework first and learn about the breed that interests them before acquiring a dog. Some breeds tend to bark more than others, or have louder or shriller voices. If a barking dog is not compatible with the person's tolerance level, lifestyle or living arrangement, then the person should consider a different pet. Most important, people must understand from the onset that dogs require a lot of time, training, socialization and play activities, starting from when they are puppies and continuing throughout their lives. Barking problems are often the result of a lack of one or more of these necessities.

Among the many options that may be tried to manage excessive barking problems are socialization, training classes and behavior modification methods. These require time and dedication. Many dog trainers offer these services, as do veterinarians specializing in animal behavior. The success or failure of behavior modification techniques varies among individual animals, trainers, behavioral counselors and the dedication of the owner.

As with any behavior problem, prevention is much easier than correction or modification.

To be successful in training your dog to do anything you will need the following:

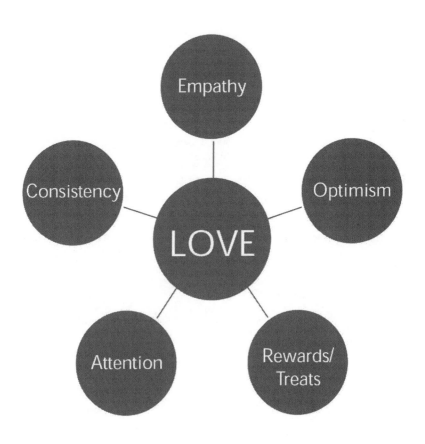

STEP 15:

Controlling Yourself

To be successful in controlling anything in this world whether it is your job, your education, your family including your DOG, you first must be in control of yourself!

Before applying any of the tools you have read in this book with your dog, first check yourself by using this simple questionnaire:

1. Do you have empathy for others including your dog?   Yes / No

2. Are you an optimist when you view your life with your dog?   Yes / No

3. Do you do things with consistency and can you see yourself being consistent with your dog?   Yes / No

4. Do you feel your canine deserves positive attention and are you willing to provide the kind of attention he/she needs?   Yes / No

5. Do you reward your canine regularly? Do you feel they reward you in return?   Yes / No

6. Do you have intense feelings of affection for the canines in your life?   Yes / No

How did you do? This quick questionnaire was just to get you in the right mindset before you begin your "new" relationship with your canine.

Always remember, your dog views life in photos, you should try the same. If you are not satisfied with the current photos you have in your files, make new ones!

Greet your canine with a smile and a very energetic YES!

By using the tools that lay throughout the pages of this book, you can control your dog in any environment, but first you must keep yourself in control!

Love is the center of it all! Show your canine love by showing him what is expected and he in return will show you that you are the center of his world! No squirrel, open door, or treat will take his attention off you because you are the leader of the pack.

Made in the USA
Middletown, DE
11 August 2016